BARRE
CHORDS

by Adam Perlmutter

ISBN 0-634-05440-6

HAL•LEONARD®
CORPORATION
7777 W. BLUEMOUND RD. P.O. BOX 13819 MILWAUKEE, WI 53213

Copyright © 2004 by HAL LEONARD CORPORATION
International Copyright Secured   All Rights Reserved

For all works contained herein:
Unauthorized copying, arranging, adapting, recording or public performance is an infringement of copyright.
Infringers are liable under the law.

Visit Hal Leonard Online at
www.halleonard.com

CONTENTS

CHAPTER 4

CHAPTER 5

CHAPTER 6

APPENDIX

What Are Barre Chords?

No, contrary to the old joke, they're not chords that you only play at your local pub. But you can bet you'll hear plenty of them there—or anywhere else the guitar is played! The barre chord is a staple in all styles of guitar playing, because it's the most practical way to access almost all the chord voicings you'll ever need.

Barre chords are moveable chord shapes that you can easily shift around the guitar's neck. In a barre chord, a single finger holds down (or *bars*) two or more strings at the same fret position on the fretboard. When you know the essential barre chord shapes, you can quickly shift from one to the next without much re-positioning.

If you haven't already played some barre chords, be warned: They might hurt a bit at first—they might even tear up a little skin on your fret-hand fingers. Stick with it, though; the calluses will come and the muscles will strengthen. Once you've mastered that first F barre chord, the rest will come easily. You'll soon see that with just a few shapes, you can strum through hundreds of songs—from blues, to folk, to rock, and beyond. You'll also find that with barre chords, you can play your favorite songs in any key!

Chords, Scales, and Key Signatures

First, a little music theory—it can only help to understand the concepts behind what you're learning, right?

A chord of any type is said to be made up of different notes of a major scale. A typical major chord, for example, is spelled out as 1–3–5, because it contains the first (or root), third, and fifth notes of the major scale. A minor chord is spelled 1–♭3–5; it contains the first, *flatted third*, and fifth notes of the major scale. It's the *3rd* that makes a chord major or minor.

The notes in the major and minor scales determine *key signatures*. The key of a song is basically the scale on which it's based, and the notes of that scale include a certain number of sharps or flats, shown at the beginning of a line of music. In the appendix at the end of this book, the *circle of 5ths* shows the sharps and flats in any given key. (Knowing the circle of 5ths will be useful in more ways than you might imagine, far beyond this book.) The key of G major contains one sharp, F♯, so a G major scale is spelled G–A–B–C–D–E–F♯.

The formula for a major chord is 1–3–5, so looking at the notes of the G major scale above, we can deduce that a G chord is spelled G–B–D; a minor chord is 1–♭3–5, so a G minor chord is G–B♭–D. The appendix also contains a chord construction chart, a handy reference of the chord spellings in this book (and some chords found elsewhere). And if this music theory confounds you, don't worry; the main goal is for you to learn the shapes and sounds of barre chords, and their applications in a variety of styles. So let's get to it!

Check your guitar's open strings against the first CD track for tuning:

TRACK 1  STANDARD TUNING (low to high): E–A–D–G–B–E

CHAPTER 1

The Basic Barre

Before we play some barre chords, let's check out the barre itself. Pick a fret, any fret. Then bar strings 1–2 at that fret:

Make sure you're pressing down evenly, so that both notes ring clearly without any buzzing.

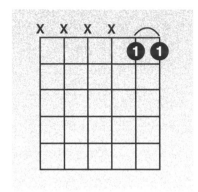

Next, do the same thing on strings 1–3. Then repeat the process, covering four, five, and finally all six strings at the same fret.

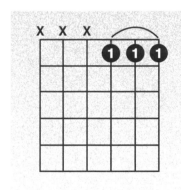  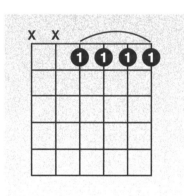 

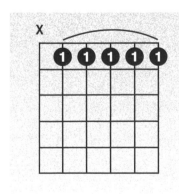  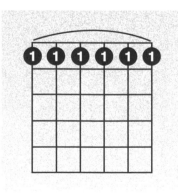 

Try this at different places up and down the neck. It will be harder to form a barre in the lower regions, so aim to clearly sound all six strings at the first fret.

The E Major Shape

And now for your first "real" barre chord. The most common barre chord shape is called an E major-type. It derives from a first-position open E chord, which you've undoubtedly seen or played already. In order to see how an open E chord transforms into a barre chord, try fingering an open E like this, without the index finger:

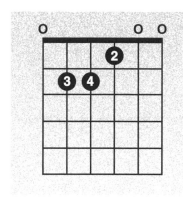 

Now slide each of the fretted notes up by one half step (one fret), and bar across the first fret with your index finger:

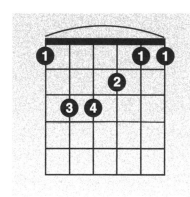 

You've got an F major barre chord! Play each note separately and make sure that it sounds clean; if necessary, apply extra pressure to the first, second, and sixth strings.

The chord spelling for this shape is 1–5–1–3–5–1 (from the lowest string to the highest); it contains three roots, two 5ths, and a 3rd. Here's the cool part: You can use that same E-based shape to create a bunch of different chords across the fretboard. All, of course, are major chords rooted on the sixth string. Each one is named after the root note of its sixth-string position.

The figure below is simple—just play the F major barre chord, and move it up one fret at a time. Do this up and down the neck, saying the name of each chord as you play it. Then play the shape at random locations and try to name the chords you form.

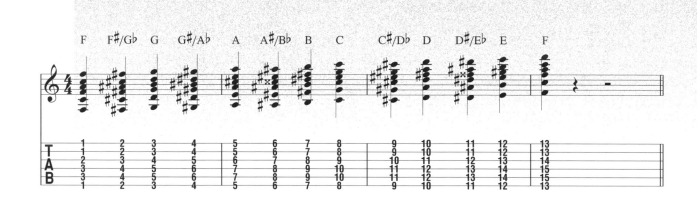

From this palette, you can draw many chord progressions, like the F major I–IV–I–V pattern below. Keep using the same E-type barre throughout, and slide up or down as indicated to access the chord changes.

Use the suggested strum patterns: The staple-looking symbol represents a downstroke (toward the floor), while the "V" shape calls for an upstroke (toward the ceiling). Practice slowly, and gradually increase the tempo until you can smoothly shift between the chords at the same moderately fast tempo as on the CD.

TRACK 2

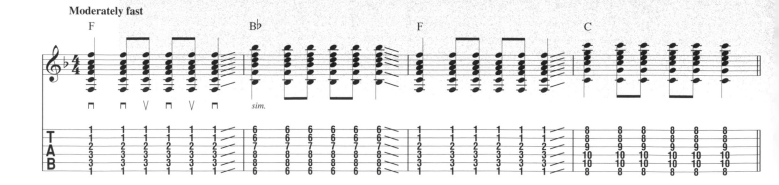

Here's the ultimate example of E major-type barre chords: the intro to the Ventures' surf classic "Walk Don't Run." The same barre shape leads into an open E chord—play it with the same fingering you learned earlier (without the first finger). Eighth-note rests in the first measure give you plenty of time to switch between chords.

TRACK 3

Walk Don't Run

By Johnny Smith

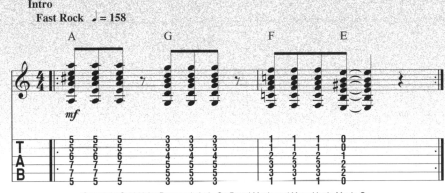

Copyright © 1960 by Peermusic Ltd., On Board Music and Mesa Verde Music Co.
Copyright Renewed
All Rights Administered by Peermusic Ltd.
International Copyright Secured   All Rights Reserved

The next example is a British Invasion-style romp in the style of the Yardbirds and The Who. It makes the most of a simple A–G progression.

In the first three measures, the dots underneath the notes call for the notes to be shortened, or *staccato*. You can do this by lifting your fret hand off the frets (but not off the strings) after you play each chord—listen to the CD to hear this effect.

TRACK 4

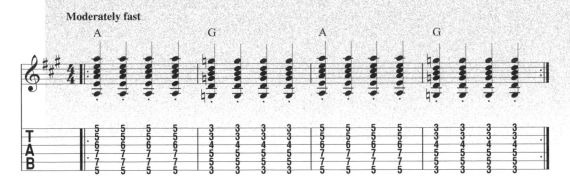

The E Minor Shape

E minor-type barre chords are also based on an open chord shape. Try this fingering for an open E minor chord:

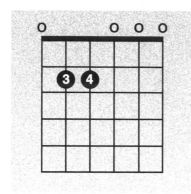 

Then slide up one fret and add your first finger to form the F minor barre chord.

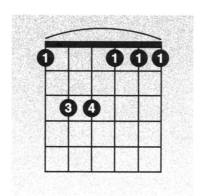 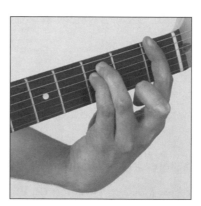

Play each note separately to make sure they sound clean; you might have to apply extra force to the first, second, third, and sixth strings. The formula for the E minor shape is 1–5–1–♭3–5–1: three roots, two 5ths, and a flatted 3rd.

Notice how you can easily turn any E-type barre chord into an E minor-type: just remove your middle finger!

Play these minor barre chords up and down the neck, and say the chords' names as you play them. With enough practice like this, you'll be able to name any chord rooted on any given sixth-string fret, instantly.

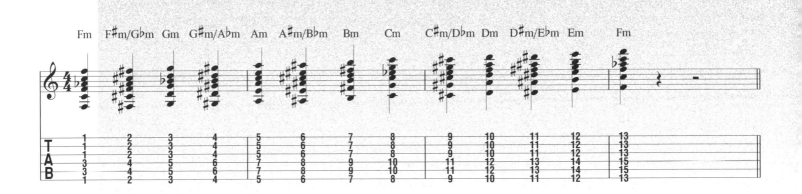

The main riff for Tom Petty's "Refugee" uses an F♯ minor barre chord with open A5 and E chords. Keep the F♯ minor chord down for the first three beats, then lift your ring finger to fret the single note G♯ on the fourth beat. Use your index finger to bar the E and A notes on the A5 chord.

TRACK 5

Refugee

Words and Music by Tom Petty and Mike Campbell

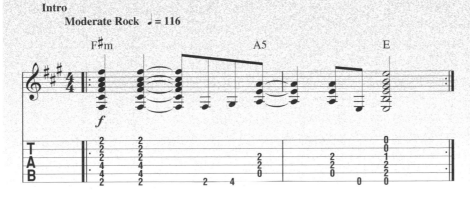

Copyright © 1979 ALMO MUSIC CORP.
All Rights Reserved   Used by Permission

The next example uses minor and major barre chords: Bm, A, and G. Hold each one down for a full measure. Pick the single notes in downstrokes, and strum the chords in upstrokes. Be sure to pay attention to the staccato dots.

TRACK 6

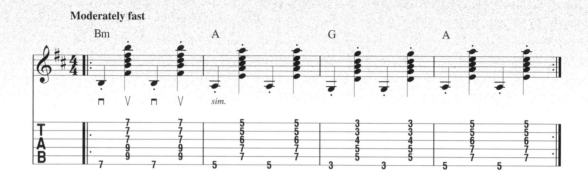

The Spin Doctors' "Two Princes" includes those same chords, plus a D major barre chord at the tenth fret. The X's in the notation and tablature show *fret-hand muting*. This is a muffled sound you get by picking while lifting you fingers off the frets—but not off the strings. Make sure no open strings ring out. While you're strumming the muted strings, you can be moving your fret hand (without lifting it) to the next chord position.

TRACK 7

Two Princes

Words and Music by Spin Doctors

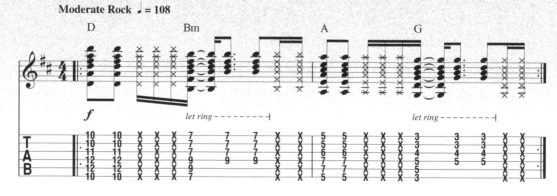

Copyright © 1991 Sony/ATV Songs LLC and Mow B'Jow Music
All Rights Administered by Sony/ATV Music Publishing, 8 Music Square West, Nashville, TN 37203
International Copyright Secured   All Rights Reserved

CHAPTER 2

The A Major Shape

Let's move up to chords rooted on the fifth string, starting with the A major type. Try this fingering for an open A chord:

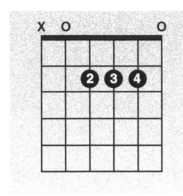

Then transfer everything up one fret to form a B♭ barre chord. This shape will be a little easier to play than the E-types, because it only involves five strings. Your middle, ring, and pinky fingers do most of the work.

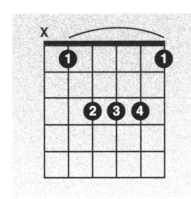
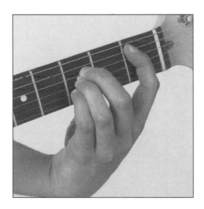

Make sure each note sounds buzz-free; pay particular attention to the first and fifth strings. The formula for A major-type chords is 1–5–1–3–5: two roots, two 5ths, and a 3rd.

Here are two alternate fingerings for the A major shape. The first removes the index-finger barre, leaves out the first string, and adds a ring finger barre on the top three notes:

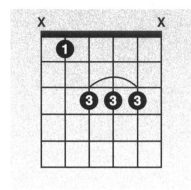 

The second, trickier fingering uses two barres at once: bar the first and fifth strings with your index finger, and the middle strings with your ring finger. In order to hear the first string, you'll need to elevate the middle knuckle of your ring finger, so you're not muting it.

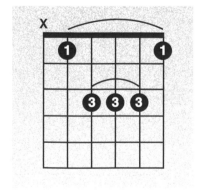 

Now acquaint yourself with these A major-type barre chords. Experiment with all three fingerings.

This I–♭III progression in C is made up of four-note, A-type barre chords. Hold the shape at fret 3 during the first measure, and at fret 6 during the second measure.

TRACK 8

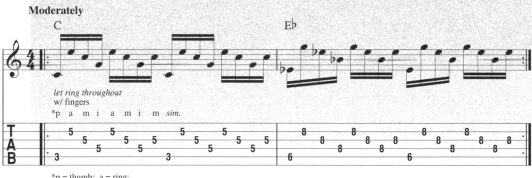

For an extra challenge, try articulating the figure with fingerpicking. As indicated by the letters under the staff, use your thumb on the fifth string, your ring finger on the second, your middle finger on the third, and your index finger on the fourth. Try to pick all the notes evenly, and let each chord ring throughout.

"American Woman"—which you may know from the Guess Who's original or Lenny Kravitz's cover—features a progression of B, D, and E barre chords. Use the same fingering as on the last figure.

Notice the *syncopation*, or accenting of the weak beats: Count *"One-ee-and-a, two-ee-and-a, three-ee-and-a, four-ee-and-a,"* etc. On each second beat, a chord will be struck on the "two," the "and," and the "a;" on the first measure's third beat, an E chord will be struck on the "ee" and the "and."

TRACK 9

American Woman

Written by Burton Cummings, Randy Bachman, Gary Peterson and Jim Kale

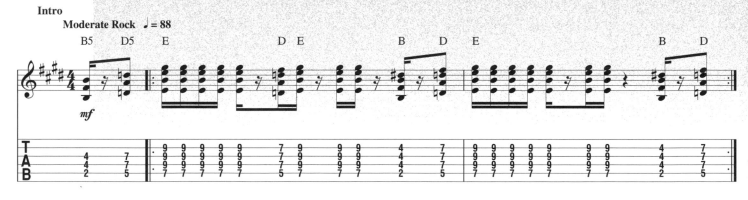

© 1970 (Renewed 1998) SHILLELAGH MUSIC (BMI)/Administered by BUG MUSIC
All Rights Reserved   Used by Permission

Judas Priest's "Living After Midnight" features those same voicings and an open A chord.

Living After Midnight

Words and Music by Glenn Tipton, Rob Halford and K.K. Downing

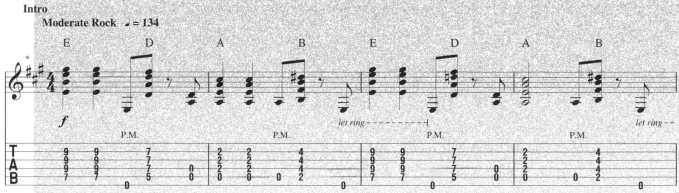

*Key signature denotes E Mixolydian.

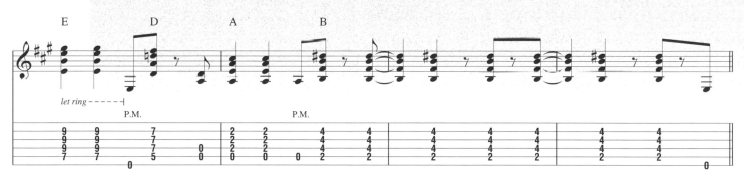

© 1980 EMI APRIL MUSIC INC., CREWGLEN LTD., EBONYTREE LTD. and GEARGATE LTD.
All Rights Controlled and Administered by EMI APRIL MUSIC INC.
All Rights Reserved   International Copyright Secured   Used by Permission

Tracy Chapman's "Give Me One Reason" puts barre chords to good use in a 12-bar blues progression in F#. For each F# chord, hold down the full, six-string E-type shape while you alternate between the sixth-string bass note and the higher triad on strings 2–4. Hold the four-note A-type shape while you play the roots and triads of the B and C# chords. When you shift from the B chord to the C# chord in measures 2 and 6, do it on the "and" of beat 2. Notice how the open string at the end of each measure makes it easier to switch chords.

Give Me One Reason

TRACK 11

Words and Music by Tracy Chapman

© 1996 EMI APRIL MUSIC INC. and PURPLE RABBIT MUSIC
All Rights Controlled and Administered by EMI APRIL MUSIC INC.
All Rights Reserved   International Copyright Secured   Used by Permission

Eric Clapton's dangerous "Cocaine" riff features E and D barre chords flanked by single-note lines from the E minor pentatonic scale (E–G–A–B–D). On the first beat, the E chord's root is reinforced with the open sixth string. In measure 2, hold down the fifth-fret notes with your index finger and the seventh-fret notes with your ring finger.

The arches (or *slurs*) connecting the noteheads and tab numbers in measure 3 represent *hammer-ons*. On the first one, strike the open sixth string, then "hammer" your index finger on the fifth-fret A without picking. Then pick that fifth-fret A again, and hammer your ring finger on the seventh-fret B. Strive for a smooth, connected sound on both sets of notes.

Notice the *legato slide* on beat 4 of the last measure. Just fret the seventh-fret E with your ring finger, pick it, and quickly slide down two frets to the fifth-fret D.

Cocaine

Words and Music by J. J. Cale

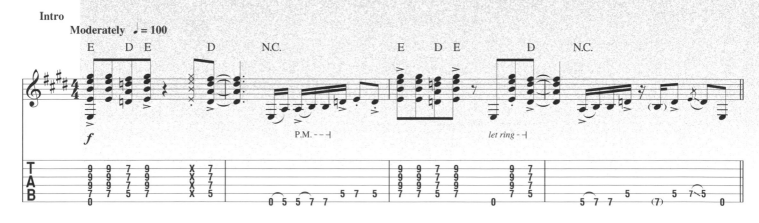

Copyright © 1975 (Renewed) AUDIGRAM MUSIC
A Division of AUDIGRAM, INC., P.O. Box 22635, Nashville, TN 37202
All Rights Reserved   Used by Permission

The A Minor Shape

The A minor-type barre chord uses the same fingering as the E major shape, moved "up a string." Start with this open A minor fingering:

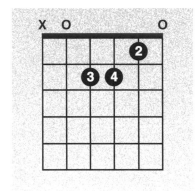

Now move it up by a half step, barring at the first fret to create a B♭ minor chord. As before, make sure the chord sounds clear: Isolate and revive any deadened pitches before moving on.

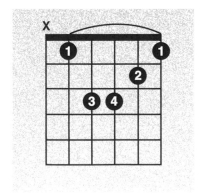
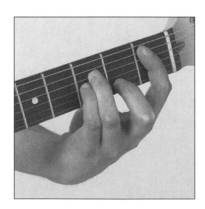

This chord shape is constructed 1–5–1–♭3–5: two roots, two 5ths, and a minor 3rd.

Play and recite the names of all the minor barre chords rooted on the 5th string:

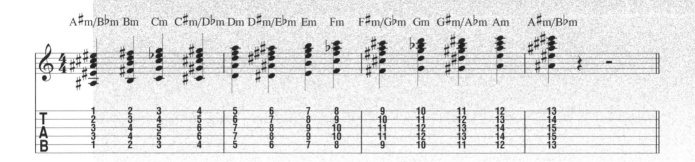

Let's put this new shape to use in some examples with both major and minor chords. Pat Benatar's '80s rock classic, "Hit Me with Your Best Shot," incorporates E, C#m, and B barre chords—all rooted on the 5th string. There's also an open A chord; bar the top three notes of it with your index finger.

To get the syncopation down, count *"one-and, two-and, three-and, four-and"* throughout. In the first and third measures, the A and C# chords fall on the "ands" of beats 2 and 4, respectively.

TRACK 13

Hit Me with Your Best Shot

Words and Music by Eddie Schwartz

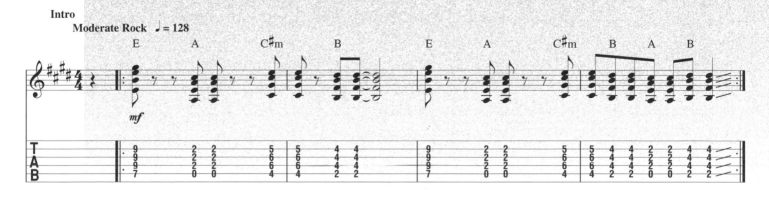

Copyright © 1978, 1980 Sony/ATV Songs LLC
All Rights Administered by Sony/ATV Music Publishing, 8 Music Square West, Nashville, TN 37203
International Copyright Secured   All Rights Reserved

In "Sultans of Swing," Dire Straits guitarist Mark Knopfler plays a i–♭VII–♭VI–V progression with roots along on the fifth string. For the barre chords, use the familiar A major and A minor shapes.

On the open A chord, use your index, middle, and ring fingers to fret the fourth, third, and second strings, respectively. To form the A7 in measure 4, simply lift your middle finger, revealing the open third string. (You'll learn more about 7th chords later.) Also, note that in the first and second measures, a chord change occurs on the "and" of beat 4.

Sultans of Swing
Words and Music by Mark Knopfler

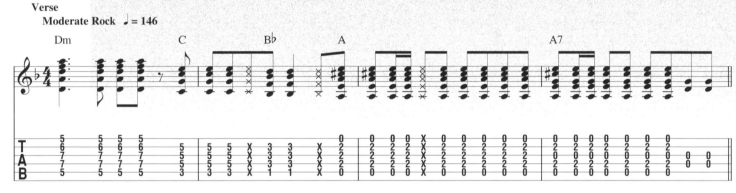

Copyright © 1978 Straitjacket Songs Ltd.
International Copyright Secured   All Rights Reserved

This I–iii–♭VII–ii progression, which you might call "Dylanesque," features both E major- and A minor-type barre chords. Use the suggested pick strokes. Notice how the strategically placed fret-hand mutes loan you time to transfer between chord shapes.

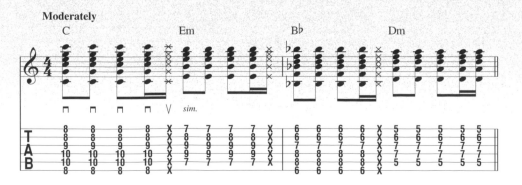

CHAPTER 3
The Esus4 Shape

Once you have the basic major and minor shapes under your fingers, you'll be ready for some new chord types. Let's start with 6th string rooted suspended 4th (or *sus4*) chords. In a sus4 chord, a 4th takes the place of a 3rd, so the chord is constructed 1–4–5. The sus4 shape shown here (1–3–1–4) is the same as the A-type major shape, moved "down a string."

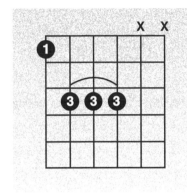

A suspended 4th has a tendency to resolve to a 3rd, as shown in this G major I–IV progression. The G and C chords are both an E-type shape, in which the index finger frets the lowest note but doesn't bar the highest two notes.

TRACK 16

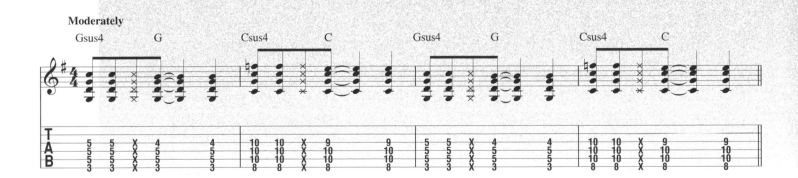

By contrast, Nirvana's "Smells Like Teen Spirit" features *unresolved* sus4 chords and A-type barre chords. There's another cool chord switching technique in the last measure: While your fingers relocate, you can strum the open strings to maintain momentum.

Smells Like Teen Spirit

Words and Music by Kurt Cobain, Chris Novoselic and David Grohl

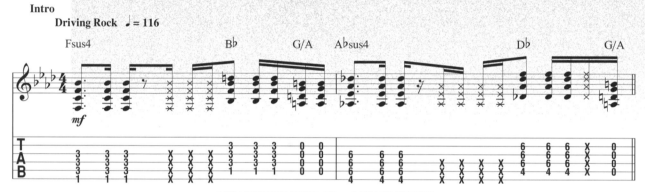

© 1991 EMI VIRGIN SONGS, INC. and THE END OF MUSIC
All Rights Controlled and Administered by EMI VIRGIN SONGS, INC.
All Rights Reserved   International Copyright Secured   Used by Permission

Here's another sus4 fingering rooted on the sixth string. Here, the thumb is wrapped around the neck to fret the root note while muting the fifth string:

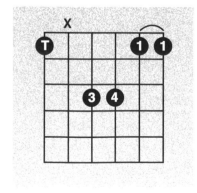

While we're getting the thumb involved, here's a new fingering—one favored by Jimi Hendrix—for E major-type barre chords:

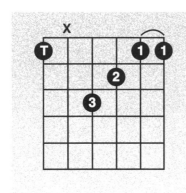 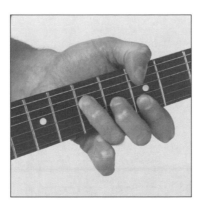

The Who's Pete Townshend uses both of these fingerings on "Pinball Wizard," from the rock opera *Tommy*. Articulate this with aggressive 16th-note strums, and accent every third note on the first three beats of both measures—as shown by the accent marks (>).

Pinball Wizard

Words and Music by Pete Townshend

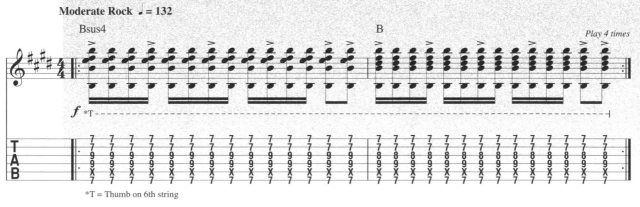

*T = Thumb on 6th string

Copyright © 1969 by Towser Tunes, Inc., ABKCO Music and Fabulous Music Ltd.
Copyright Renewed
All Rights for Towser Tunes, Inc. Administered by BMG Music Publishing International
All Rights for BMG Music Publishing International in the U.S. Administered by Careers-BMG Music Publishing, Inc.
International Copyright Secured   All Rights Reserved

The Eadd9 Shape

Take an E major-type barre chord and raise its fourth-string root note by a whole step (two frets). What you get is an add9 chord, which expands a major chord with its 9th (or 2nd):

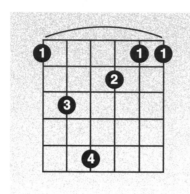

This shape requires a bit of a stretch, so try it in higher positions (where the frets are closer together), and proceed down the neck until you can play an Fadd9 chord clearly and comfortably. The formula for this Eadd9-type chord shape is 1–5–9(2)–3–5–1.

Here's a figure that starts on a Dadd9 chord and travels chromatically (by half step) down to a Gadd9 chord. Try using *hybrid picking*—a combination of pick and fingers. Use the suggested pick and middle finger plucks, or experiment with some of your own pick/hand combinations.

TRACK 19

The Asus4 Shape

An A-type sus4 chord is pretty straightforward; it just adds a pinky to the basic major shape.

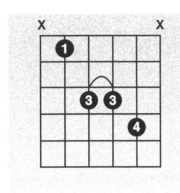

The Romantics' "What I Like About You" includes Esus4 and Asus4 chords. On the Asus4, bar the middle two notes with your index finger, and use your ring finger on the third-fret D. The A/C♯ chord is a type of *slash chord*, in which the lowest note (to the right of the slash) is something other than the root; in this case it's C♯, the 3rd of the A chord. Fret it with your ring ringer, and fret the 3rd and 2nd strings with your index and middle fingers, respectively.

TRACK 20

What I Like About You

Words and Music by Michael Skill, Wally Palamarchuk and James Marinos

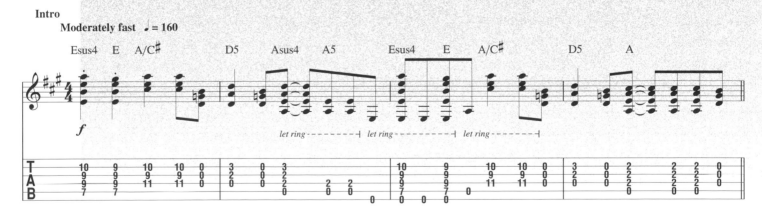

© 1979 EMI APRIL MUSIC INC.
All Rights Reserved   International Copyright Secured   Used by Permission

In the spirit of Eddie Van Halen, this example pits A- and Asus4-type barre chords against an open E *pedal tone*—a note that stays constant under moving chords. The letters "P.M." under the staff stand for *palm muting*. Rest your hand near the guitar's bridge, and press down slightly, so the open E string gives you that "chunk" sound. Don't put on too much pressure, or the string will sound out of tune; listen to the CD for the desired effect.

Throughout the example, count *"one-ee-an-a, two-ee-and-a, three-ee-and-a, four-ee-and-a,"* etc. Note that a chord falls on the "a" of each first and third beat.

Try playing this figure with all downstrokes to accentuate the "chunk."

TRACK 21

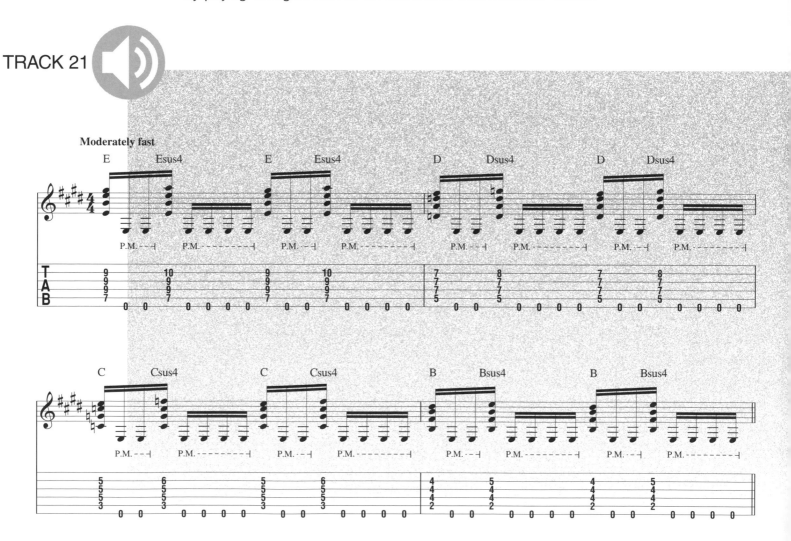

The Asus2 Shape

Another common barre chord is the Asus2-type. In a sus2 chord (1–2–5), the suspended second takes the place of the 3rd. You can form an Asus2-type chord by removing your middle finger from any A minor-type; the arrangement is 1–5–1–2–5.

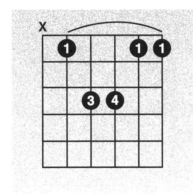
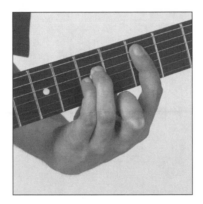

Now try this new fingering in a C major I–IV–V–IV progression, reminiscent of Jimi Hendrix covering a Bob Dylan tune.

TRACK 22

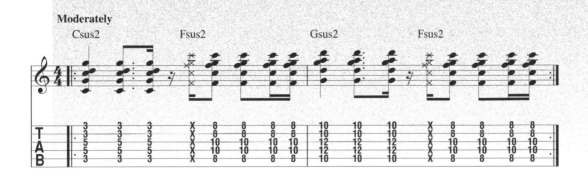

Seen on the next page, the Police's "Every Breath You Take" is constructed of E- and A-type add9 and sus2 chords. To form the F#m(add9) chord, simply remove your middle finger from the third string of the Eadd9-type shape. For the Dsus2, use this shape:

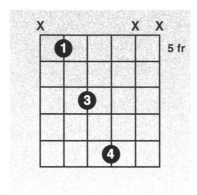

And use this shape for the E5:

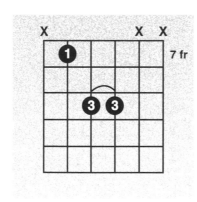

Note that this last shape is actually a *power chord*—a sonority containing only a root and a 5th (in any arrangement of roots and 5ths).

Use a palm mute throughout this eight-measure excerpt of "Every Breath You Take." Practice slowly, gradually increasing the tempo until you can smoothly shift between chord shapes at the speed of the CD.

TRACK 23

Every Breath You Take

Music and Lyrics by Sting

*Chord symbols reflect implied harmony.

© 1983 G.M. SUMNER
Administered by EMI MUSIC PUBLISHING LIMITED
All Rights Reserved   International Copyright Secured   Used by Permission

CHAPTER 4
Dominant 7th Barre Chords

Paul McCartney once said in an interview that one day during the Beatles' formative years, they rode a train for hours just to visit a guitar guru who knew how to finger a B7 chord! Look no further than this book to learn all types of 7th chords.

A *dominant 7th* chord, as it's formally called, is a major triad with a flatted 7th (1–3–5–♭7). Start with this open E7 fingering:

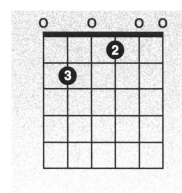

Now raise it by a half step to form the basic barre shape (formula: 1–5–♭7–3–5–1).

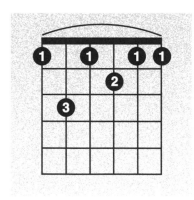
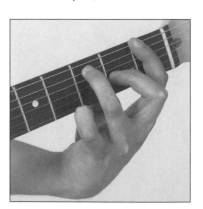

By now, if you've been practicing diligently, you should be able to fret these shapes cleanly without too much trouble.

Once you've gotten to know the E7-type barre chord in assorted locations, try playing this 12-bar blues form. Follow the staccato markings by releasing pressure on your fret-hand fingers after you strum each chord.

TRACK 24

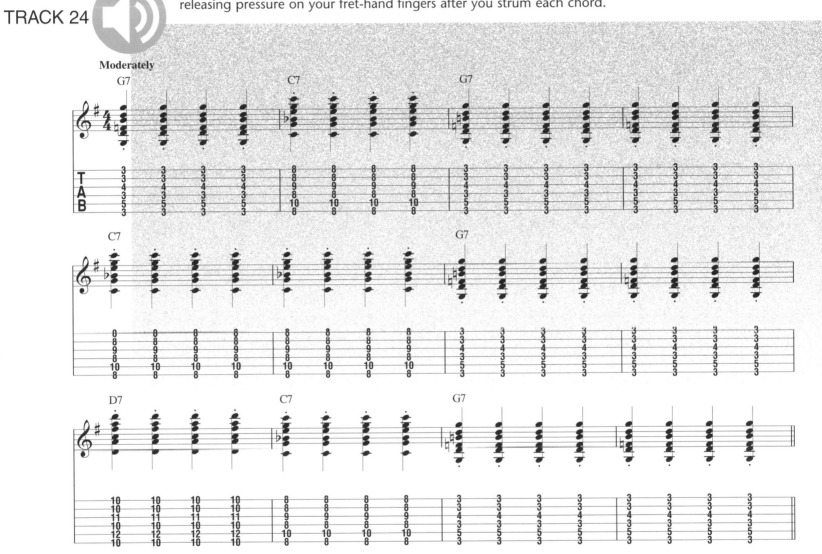

In an alternate E7-type barre chord, the pinky finger reinforces the lowered 7th, creating this shape:

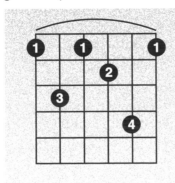 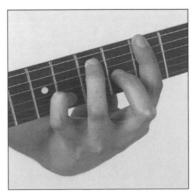

This pinky-reinforced voicing might sound a little cooler than the previous one, due to the major 2nd interval between the highest two strings.

Once you're totally comfortable with the newer shape, try this F blues chorus. Play the chord stabs staccato, and go longer on the root-5th bass notes to create a lively rhythm figure.

TRACK 25

Now for the A7-type barre chord. First, play this fingering for an open A7 chord:

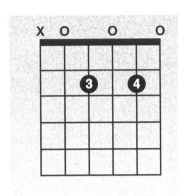 

Then move the shape up and add the first-finger barre for a closed B♭7 chord (spelled 1–5–♭7–3–5).

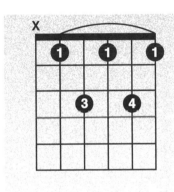 

Let's incorporate these A7-type chords in a *turnaround*—a group of chords that takes you back to the beginning of a repeated progression.

Measures 1–2 of this example are a typical blues turnaround; they function as the last two measures of a 12-bar blues in B♭, bringing it all home to a B♭7 chord in the third measure. In the second half of measure 1, the progression starts on D♭7 and chromatically returns to the I chord (B♭7).

TRACK 26

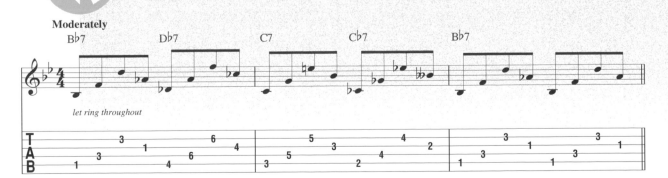

Here's another B♭ turnaround—this one is a I–♭III–♭VI–V pattern inspired by jazz:

TRACK 27

Because of the distances between the chords' roots, this example can be played more efficiently with a combination of E7- and A7-type chords:

TRACK 28

Minor 7th Barre Chords

A *minor 7th* chord is a minor triad with a flatted 7th, shown as "m7" in chord symbols. By now, you probably understand how barre chords are derived from first-position open shapes, so let's go straight to some closed, moveable fingerings. Here are two fingerings for full Em7-type shapes:

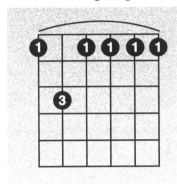 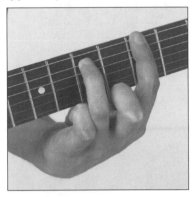

The second fingering has that cool major 2nd interval between the top two notes:

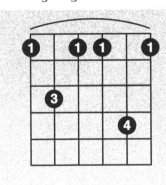 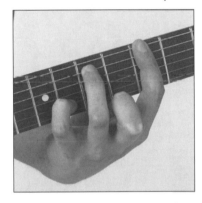

Spend some time to get comfortable with each of these fingerings; play them at different positions up and down the guitar neck.

Here's a funky i–iv progression in F minor with both of the full Em7-type shapes. Maintain the first fingering throughout, adding your pinky finger to the second string during the first half of each beat 2, and for the duration of each beat 3. Use alternating strokes.

TRACK 29

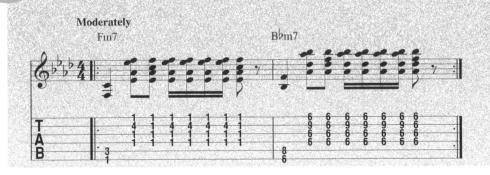

Here are two different fingerings for a four-note variation of the Em7-type voicing; jazz cats favor the first...

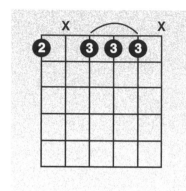
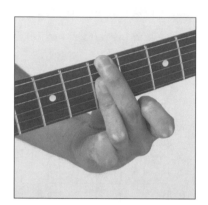

...and the second is useful for blues players.

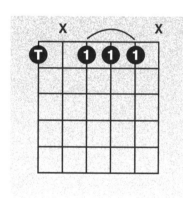
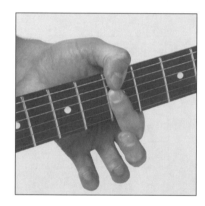

Again, play these shapes all around the guitar neck to get familiar with them.

Here's a blues version of the same progression you last played (expanded to two measures per chord). Use the thumb-rooted Em7-type fingering. On the Fm7 chord, use your index finger for each third-fret note, and on the B♭m7 chord use your ring finger for each eighth-fret note.

The curved arrow and "1/4" in the tab calls for a slight, *quarter-step bend*: Strike the string, then gently pull it toward the floor with your fret-hand finger, for an expressive vocal-like quality.

The wavy lines in measures 2 and 4 represent fret-hand *vibrato*, another emotive technique created by rapidly moving your finger to shake the note. Vibrato is very personalized; experimentation is the only way to find your own vibrato style.

TRACK 30

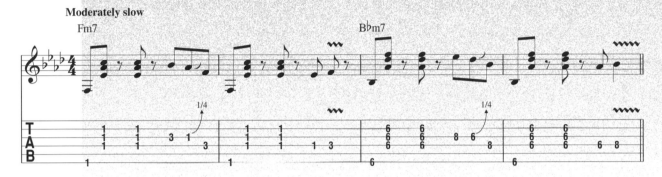

Here's a figure inspired by classic funk riffs. Here our i–iv progression is enhanced by single-note lines. On each chord, hold the basic shape in place, as you add your pinky to fret the second string note on each fourth beat. Be sure to count "One-ee-and-a, two-ee-and-a, three-ee-and-a, four-ee-and-a," etc. Note that on the first beat of each measure, the second chord stab falls on the "a."

TRACK 31

Here are two Am7-type barre chord shapes. The first, most common shape is basically an A minor-type with the pinky finger removed:

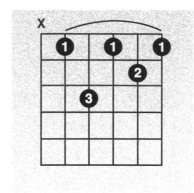 

The second shape reinforces the ♭7 with the pinky on the first string:

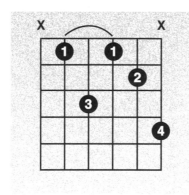 

Play both with assorted roots up and down the neck, and try making some of your own progressions based on them.

In the reggae-inflected Police tune, "The Bed's Too Big Without You," guitarist Andy Summers plays Am and Bm chords, followed by a pulled-off Em7 at the seventh fret. On the Am and Bm chords, play long on the beats and short on the "ands." Each time the Em7 is struck, pull the second- and fourth-string notes off to the index-finger barre.

The Bed's Too Big Without You

Music and Lyrics by Sting

© 1979 G.M. SUMNER
Administered by EMI MUSIC PUBLISHING LIMITED
All Rights Reserved   International Copyright Secured   Used by Permission

On Weezer's "Say It Ain't So," secret metalhead Rivers Cuomo does the opposite—he hammers onto a C#m7 from the index-finger barre. The G#add#9 and A chords are both partial E-type barre chords; the open B string at the end of measure 3 adds some great dissonance.

Say It Ain't So

Words and Music by Rivers Cuomo

Copyright © 1994 E.O. Smith Music
International Copyright Secured   All Rights Reserved

Major 7th Barre Chords

A *major 7th* chord is a major triad with a *major* (rather than dominant) 7th. (Its construction is 1–3–5–7). These pretty-sounding chords are most commonly heard in jazz and pop.

Here's the fingering for Emaj7-type chords:

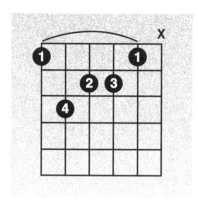 

And here's the Amaj7-type:

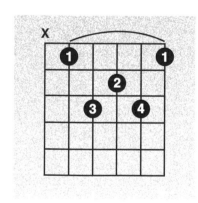 

Take a little while to acquaint yourself with these new chords.

Here's a Bossa Nova-style I–♭II vamp. To play it, take the Amaj7-type shape, and extend the barre to cover the sixth string. Use fingerpicking, and let every note ring out.

TRACK 34

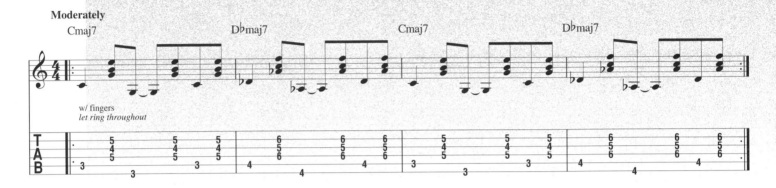

Here's a jazzy I–♭III–♭VI–♭II turnaround in the key of F major. It's built from both Emaj7- and Amaj7-type shapes.

TRACK 35

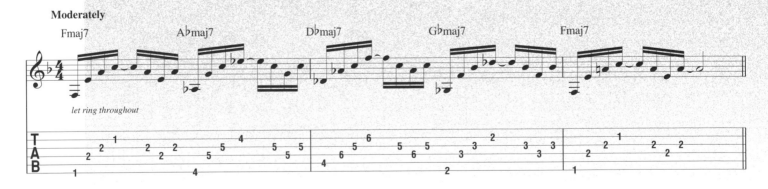

Suspended 7th Barre Chords

7sus4 chords, also known as *suspended 7th* chords (1–4–5–♭7), will add another nice sound to your harmonic vocabulary. These are basically dominant 7th chords in which the 4th is suspended. Here is the E7sus4-type shape, spelled 1–5–♭7–4–5–1:

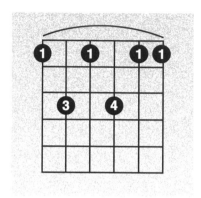 

And here's the A7sus4-type, spelled 1–5–♭7–4–5:

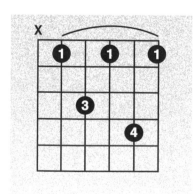 

Both of these new chord types can be found in the following I–IV–♭III–♭VI progression. Be sure to play the second chord of each measure on the "and" of beat 2.

TRACK 36

In this variation, each chord's 4th resolves down to its 3rd:

TRACK 37

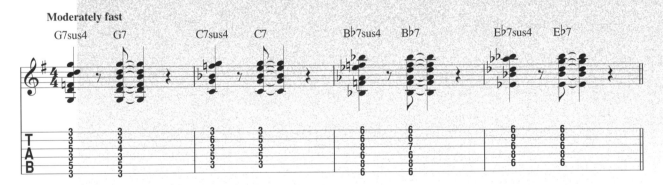

This jazzy 12-bar blues form incorporates all of the 7th chord types you've encoun- tered so far. The example's four-to-the-bar rhythm is characteristic of Freddie Green, who supported the Count Basie band with his propulsive strumming.

As suggested in the first two measures, use all downstrokes, but occasionally toss in a muted upstroke on an offbeat, as on the "and" of beat 4 in measure 1.

TRACK 38

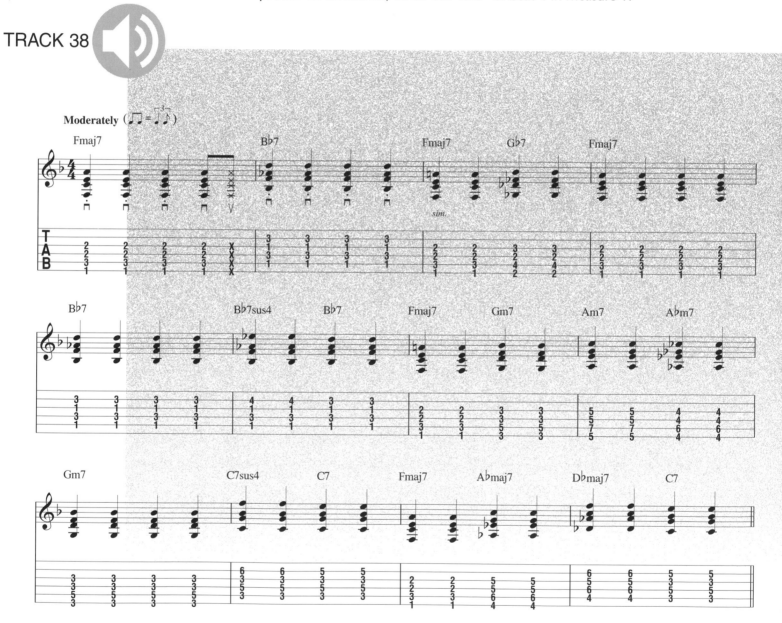

CHAPTER 5
9th Barre Chords

A dominant 9th chord, labeled simply as "9," is a dominant 7th chord with an added 9th (1–3–5–♭7–9). Here is the fingering for the 6th string-rooted version (formulized as 1–5–♭7–3–5–9):

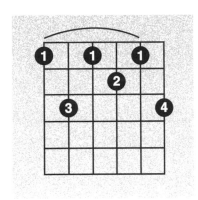

And here's the 5th string-rooted version (1–3–♭7–9–5):

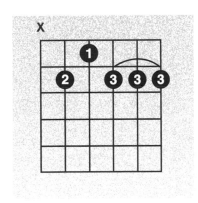

This blues-based example flanks both 9th chord shapes with single-note lines derived from the G minor pentatonic scale (G–B♭–C–D–F). Play those lines in third position: Use your index finger on each third-fret note, your ring finger on each fifth-fret note, and your pinky finger on each sixth-fret note.

TRACK 39

13th Chords

Play an A9-type shape, and add your pinky finger to the first string, two frets up from the barre. You now have a 13th chord. The construction is 1–3–5–♭7–9–11–13; this voicing contains the most essential tones: 1–3–♭7–9–13.

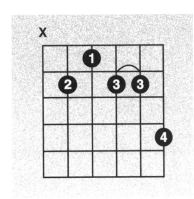

These chord types abound in the music of James Brown. In the funk opus "Get Up (I Feel Like Being) a Sex Machine," alternate chord stabs with rests and mutes, leaving plenty of room for other instruments. There's an important lesson: What you *don't* play is just as important as what you *do* play—especially in funk.

Get Up (I Feel Like Being) A Sex Machine

Words and Music by James Brown, Bobby Byrd and Ronald Lenhoff

TRACK 40

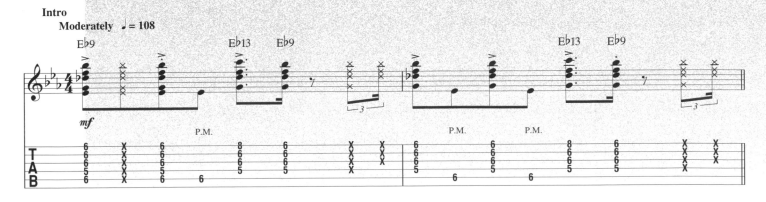

Copyright © 1970 by Dynatone Publishing Co.
Copyright Renewed
All Rights Administered by Unichappell Music Inc.
International Copyright Secured   All Rights Reserved

Minor 9th Barre Chords

A *minor 9th* chord is a minor 7th chord with an added 9th (1–3–5–♭7–9). Here is the 6th string-rooted type, constructed 1–5–♭7–♭3–5–9. This Em9-type shape can also be played with just the top four notes.

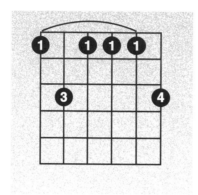

Here's the 5th string-rooted type of minor 9th chord, spelled 1–♭3–♭7–9:

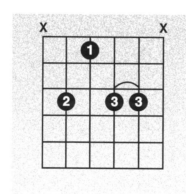

And here is an alternate, non-barred fingering for the Am9-type chord:

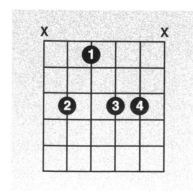

In this example, use the first Am9-type fingering for the Fm9 chord. That will leave your pinky free to finger the ninth-fret A♭ note that comes next. Play the example slowly, letting all notes ring for as long as possible.

TRACK 41

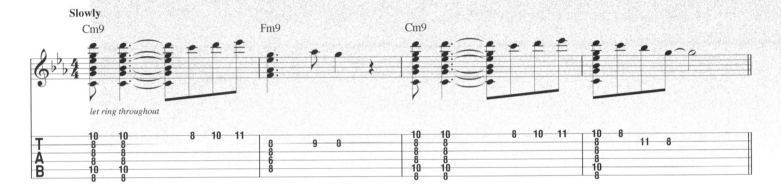

On Ozzy Osbourne's "Goodbye to Romance"—a good example of jazzy chords in a rock context—guitarist Randy Rhoads plays a sixth string-rooted Bm9 chord, and also reveals these two new fingerings for fourth string-rooted maj7 and 7sus4 chords:

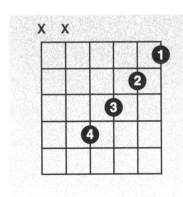 

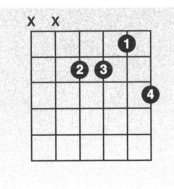 

With those shapes at hand, play through the verse figure from "Goodbye to Romance." On the Bm9 chord, the index finger only has to bar strings 1–4.

Goodbye to Romance

TRACK 42

Words and Music by John Osbourne, Robert Daisley and Randy Rhoads

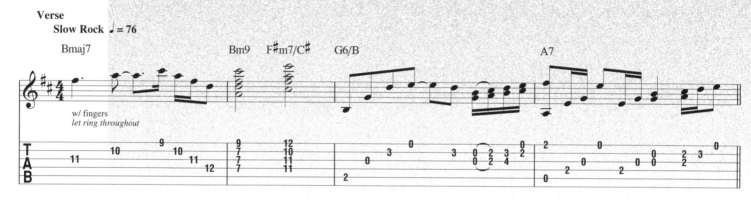

TRO - © Copyright 1981 and 1984 Essex Music International, Inc., New York and Blizzard Music, Daytona Beach, FL
International Copyright Secured
All Rights Reserved Including Public Performance for Profit
Used by Permission

CHAPTER 6
Drop D Tuning

With alternate tunings, barre chords take on entirely new shapes and sounds. Some tunings allow you to play full chords with just one finger!

The most common tuning is Drop D, often used by hard rock guitarists. Just lower your sixth string from E down a whole step to D. You can use an electronic tuner or a piano for reference, or simply match a twelfth-fret note or harmonic on the sixth string with the open fourth string. Here's a tuning track to get you started:

 TRACK 43  DROP D TUNING (LOW TO HIGH): D-A-D-G-B-E

In Drop D, you can play a power chord by simply barring the lowest two or three strings. This makes it easy to slur chords using hammer-ons, pull-offs, and slides.

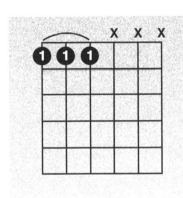 

In this example, try barring the first F5 chord on fret 3 with your index finger, the fifth-fret G5 with your ring finger, and the sixth-fret A♭5 with your pinky. On beat 4, slide from the F5 to the G5 with your index finger.

 TRACK 44

Drop D tuning:
(low to high) D-A-D-G-B-E

Moderately

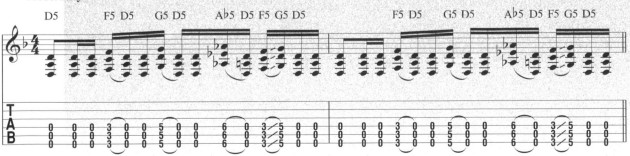

Played in the nonstandard time signature of 7/4, Soundgarden's "Spoonman" riff requires position shifts. First, bar the C5 chord with your index finger, then hammer on the twelfth-fret D5 with your ring finger. Use a ring-finger barre at the A5 chord, and fret the following G5 chord with your index finger. In a final position shift, fret the F5 and G5 chords with your index and ring fingers, respectively.

TRACK 45

Spoonman

Words and Music by Chris Cornell

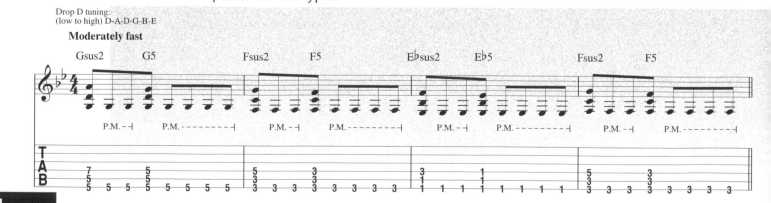

Copyright © 1994 You Make Me Sick I Make Music (ASCAP)
International Copyright Secured   All Rights Reserved

In Drop D tuning, sus2 chords are easy to play. Here's a three-note sus2 fingering, in which the 2nd (9th) is fretted with the ring finger.

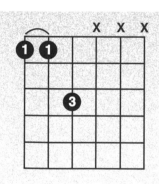

TRACK 46

In this progression, each sus2 chord resolves to a power chord; palm-muted root notes separate the two types.

Drop D tuning:
(low to high) D-A-D-G-B-E

Moderately fast

Open G Tuning

In open G tuning, you can play any major chord with a single finger by barring strings 5–1. The Rolling Stones' guitarist Keith Richards often uses this tuning, and he often removes the 6th string for simplicity's sake—but don't try this at home just yet. Just tune your sixth, fifth, and first strings down a step, to get this arrangement:

TRACK 47 OPEN G TUNING: (LOW TO HIGH) D-G-D-G-B-D

Now, barring strings 5–1 will give you a full major chord:

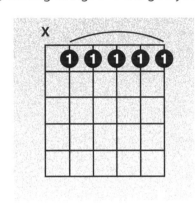 

Here's a I–♭III–IV–V progression that you can play with the index finger at the fifth, eighth, tenth, and twelfth frets.

TRACK 48

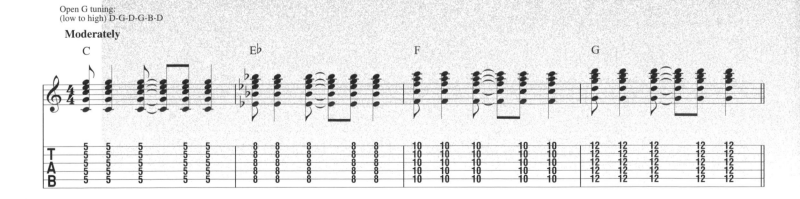

In open G tuning, a *second inversion* major chord (with the 5th in the bass) is formed with the same shape you used to create a minor 7th chord in standard tuning:

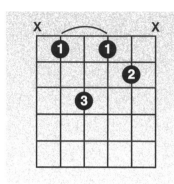
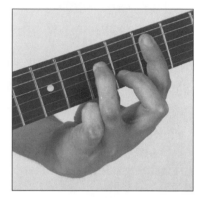

TRACK 49

Here's the same I–♭III–IV–V progression you just played, but with the new voicing in a chain of I–IV moves:

Open G tuning:
(low to high) D-G-D-G-B-D

Moderately

To play the Stones' "Start Me Up," start with a five-string barred C chord, and add fingers 1 and 3 where shown to create an Fadd2/C. The B♭5 is also an index-finger barre; add the third finger on string 4, fret 5 to turn it into a bluesy B♭6.

TRACK 50

Start Me Up

Open G tuning:
(low to high) D-G-D-G-B-D

Words and Music by Mick Jagger and Keith Richards

Moderately ♩ = 122

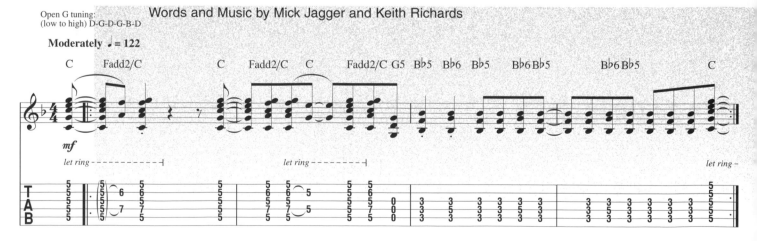

© 1981 EMI MUSIC PUBLISHING LTD.
All Rights for the U.S. and Canada Controlled and Administered by COLGEMS-EMI MUSIC INC.
All Rights Reserved   International Copyright Secured   Used by Permission

APPENDIX
Fretboard Chart

This chart displays all of the available pitches on the fretboard. Two pitches shown together are called *enharmonic*, meaning they are two different note names for the same pitch.

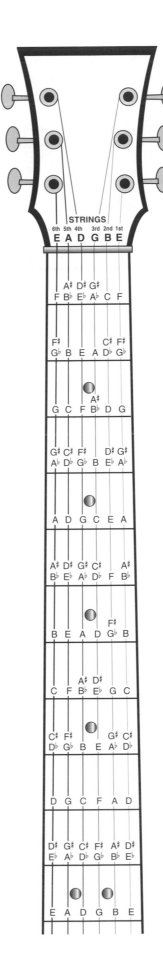

Reading Chord Diagrams

A chord diagram represents a chunk of the guitar's neck, and indicates the notes and fingerings of a particular chord, which is named on top. The horizontal lines are frets and the vertical lines symbolize strings (as if the guitar neck is pointing up). A number on the right of a frame shows the fret position; "10 fr" means the diagram starts at fret 10. In open position, you'll see a thick horizontal line designating the guitar's nut (where the neck meets the headstock). An "o" above a frame indicates an open string, and an "x" calls for a string to be muted or left unplayed. Dots on the diagram are fingerings, and a *barre*, the curvy line above the fingerings, indicates that the given strings are to be held down with the same finger. Inside the dots are numbers that explain which fret-hand fingers to use: 1=index, 2=middle, 3=ring, and 4=pinky.

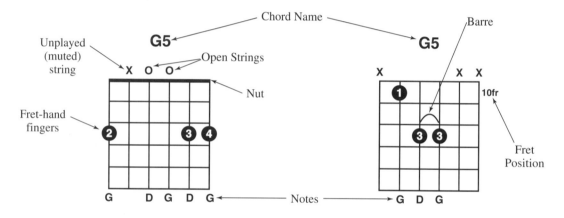

Reading Tablature

Tablature (or *tab*) is another representation of the guitar's fretboard, showing the string and fret coordinates of any note. The six horizontal lines represent strings: the bottom line is the low E-string, and the highest is the high E-string. While tablature is extremely helpful in terms of positioning, it is not meant to replace standard notation.

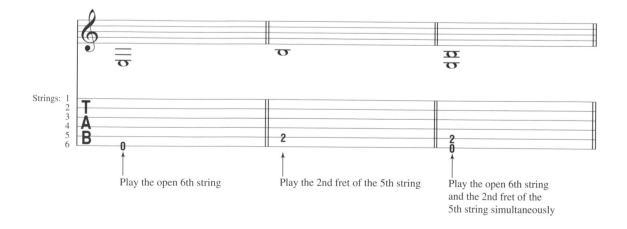

The Circle of 5ths

The *circle of fifths* is a useful tool if you want to know what chords are common within a key. Major keys line the outside of the circle; their relative minors line the inside.

Right now, the box is highlighting chords that belong to both C major and its relative A minor. To find the chords for another key, just mentally rotate the box.

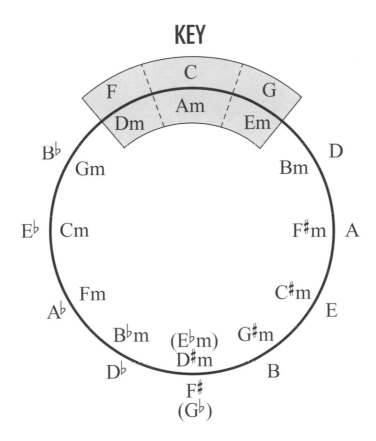

Chord Construction Chart

Chord name	Abbreviation	Chord formula
major	(none)	1 3 5
minor	m	1 ♭3 5
power chord	5	1 5
suspended 2nd	sus2	1 2 5
suspended 4th	sus4	1 4 5
dominant 7th	7th	1 3 5 ♭7
major 7th	maj7	1 3 5 7
minor 7th	m7	1 ♭3 5 ♭7
minor (major 7th)	m(maj7)	1 ♭3 5 7
dominant 9th	9	1 3 5 ♭7 9
major 9th	maj9	1 3 5 7 9
minor 9th	m9	1 ♭3 5 ♭7 9
added 9th	add9	1 3 5 9
minor added 9th	m(add9)	1 ♭3 5 9
6th	6	1 3 5 6
minor 6th	m6	1 ♭3 5 6
6th added 9th	6/9	1 3 5 6 9
minor 6th added 9th	m6/9	1 ♭3 5 6 9
7th flatted 5th	7♭5	1 3 ♭5 ♭7
7th flatted 9th	7♭9	1 3 5 ♭7 ♭9
7th sharped 9th	7♯9	1 3 5 ♭7 ♯9
7th suspended 4th	7sus4	1 4 5 ♭7
diminished	°	1 ♭3 ♭5
diminished 7th	°7	1 ♭3 ♭5 ♭♭7
half diminished	ø	1 ♭3 ♭5 ♭7
minor 7th flatted 5th	m7♭5	1 ♭3 ♭5 ♭7
Augmented	+	1 3 ♯5
Augmented 7th	+7	1 3 ♯5 ♭7
dominant 11th	11	1 3 5 ♭7 9 11
9th suspended 4th	9sus4	1 4 5 ♭7 9
minor 11th	m11	1 ♭3 5 ♭7 9 11
dominant 13th	13	1 3 5 ♭7 9 11 13

Guitar Notation Legend

Guitar Music can be notated three different ways: on a *musical staff*, in *tablature*, and in *rhythm slashes*.

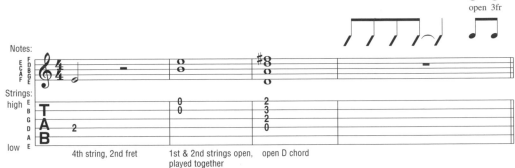

RHYTHM SLASHES are written above the staff. Strum chords in the rhythm indicated. Use the chord diagrams found at the top of the first page of the transcription for the appropriate chord voicings. Round noteheads indicate single notes.

THE MUSICAL STAFF shows pitches and rhythms and is divided by bar lines into measures. Pitches are named after the first seven letters of the alphabet.

TABLATURE graphically represents the guitar fingerboard. Each horizontal line represents a string, and each number represents a fret.

4th string, 2nd fret   1st & 2nd strings open, played together   open D chord

HALF-STEP BEND: Strike the note and bend up 1/2 step.

WHOLE-STEP BEND: Strike the note and bend up one step.

GRACE NOTE BEND: Strike the note and immediately bend up as indicated.

SLIGHT (MICROTONE) BEND: Strike the note and bend up 1/4 step.

BEND AND RELEASE: Strike the note and bend up as indicated, then release back to the original note. Only the first note is struck.

PRE-BEND: Bend the note as indicated, then strike it.

VIBRATO: The string is vibrated by rapidly bending and releasing the note with the fretting hand.

WIDE VIBRATO: The pitch is varied to a greater degree by vibrating with the fretting hand.

HAMMER-ON: Strike the first (lower) note with one finger, then sound the higher note (on the same string) with another finger by fretting it without picking.

PULL-OFF: Place both fingers on the notes to be sounded. Strike the first note and without picking, pull the finger off to sound the second (lower) note.

LEGATO SLIDE: Strike the first note and then slide the same fret-hand finger up or down to the second note. The second note is not struck.

SHIFT SLIDE: Same as legato slide, except the second note is struck.

TRILL: Very rapidly alternate between the notes indicated by continuously hammering on and pulling off.

TAPPING: Hammer ("tap") the fret indicated with the pick-hand index or middle finger and pull off to the note fretted by the fret hand.

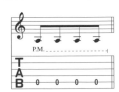

NATURAL HARMONIC: Strike the note while the fret-hand lightly touches the string directly over the fret indicated.

Harm.

PINCH HARMONIC: The note is fretted normally and a harmonic is produced by adding the edge of the thumb or the tip of the index finger of the pick hand to the normal pick attack.

P.H.

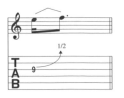

PICK SCRAPE: The edge of the pick is rubbed down (or up) the string, producing a scratchy sound.

P.S.

MUFFLED STRINGS: A percussive sound is produced by laying the fret hand across the string(s) without depressing, and striking them with the pick hand.

PALM MUTING: The note is partially muted by the pick hand lightly touching the string(s) just before the bridge.

P.M.

RAKE: Drag the pick across the strings indicated with a single motion.

rake

TREMOLO PICKING: The note is picked as rapidly and continuously as possible.

VIBRATO BAR DIVE AND RETURN: The pitch of the note or chord is dropped a specified number of steps (in rhythm) then returned to the original pitch.

w/ bar

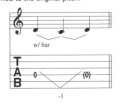

VIBRATO BAR SCOOP: Depress the bar just before striking the note, then quickly release the bar.

w/ bar

VIBRATO BAR DIP: Strike the note and then immediately drop a specified number of steps, then release back to the original pitch.

-1-

GET BETTER AT GUITAR

...with These Great Guitar Instruction Books from Hal Leonard!

DON'T FRET NOTE MAP

REVOLUTIONARY GUITAR FINGER POSITIONING GUIDE
• *created by Nicholas Ravagni*

It's never been easier to learn to play guitar! For beginners just starting out or experienced guitarists who want to learn to read music, the *Don't Fret Note Map*™ will give players the tools they need to locate notes on the guitar. This revolutionary finger positioning guide fits all electric and acoustic guitars with no adhesive or fasteners, shows the note names and locations all over the fretboard and uses a unique color-coded method to make note-reading easy. The accompanying booklet includes full instructions and four easy songs to let players practice their new-found skills!

_____00695587 ....$9.95

Also available:
DON'T FRET CHORD MAP™

REVOLUTIONARY GUITAR FINGER POSITIONING GUIDE
• *created by Nicholas Ravagni*

_____00695670 ....$9.95

GUITAR DIAL 9-1-1

50 WAYS TO IMPROVE YOUR PLAYING ... NOW!! • *by Ken Parille*

Need to breathe new life into your guitar playing? This book is your admission into the Guitar ER! You'll learn to: expand your harmonic vocabulary; improvise with chromatic notes; create rhythmic diversity; improve your agility through helpful drills; supply soulful fills; create melodic lines through chord changes; and much more! The accompanying CD includes 99 demonstration tracks.

_____00695405 Book/CD Pack.............................$16.95

GUITAR TECHNIQUES • *by Michael Mueller*

Guitar Techniques is a terrific reference and teaching companion, as it clearly defines and demonstrates how to properly execute cool moves ranging from bending, vibrato and legato to tapping, whammy bar and playing with your teeth! The CD contains 92 demonstration tracks in country, rock, pop and jazz styles. Essential techniques covered include: Fretting • Strumming • Trills • Picking • Vibrato • Tapping • Bends • Harmonics • Muting • Slides • and more.

_____00695562 Book/CD Pack.............................$14.95

THE GUITARIST'S SURVIVAL KIT

EVERYTHING YOU NEED TO KNOW TO BE A WORKING MUSICIAN
• *by Dale Turner*

From repertoire to accompaniment patterns to licks, this book is fully stocked to give you the confidence knowing you can "get by" and survive, regardless of the situation. The book covers: songs and set lists; gear; rhythm riffs in styles from blues to funk to rock to metal; lead licks in blues, country, jazz & rock styles; transposition and more. The CD features 99 demonstration tracks, and the book includes standard notation and tab.

_____00695380 Book/CD Pack.............................$14.95

LEFT-HANDED GUITAR

THE COMPLETE METHOD • *by Troy Stetina*

Attention all Southpaws: it's time to turn your playing around! We're proud to announce that our groundbreaking guitar method solely devoted to lefties is now available with a CD! Complete with photos, diagrams and grids designed especially for the left-handed player, this book/CD pack teaches fundamentals such as: chords, scales, riffs, strumming; rock, blues, fingerpicking and other styles; tuning and theory; reading standard notation and tablature; and much more!

_____00695630 Book/CD Pack...................................$14.95
_____00695247 Book Only..$9.95

PICTURE CHORD ENCYCLOPEDIA

PHOTOS & DIAGRAMS FOR 2,600 GUITAR CHORDS!

The most comprehensive guitar chord resource ever! Beginning with helpful notes on how to use the book, how to choose the best voicings and how to construct chords, this extensive, 272-page source for all playing styles and levels features five easy-to-play voicings of 44 chord qualities for each of the twelve musical keys – 2,640 chords in all! For each, there is a clearly illustrated chord frame, as well as *an actual photo* of the chord being played! Includes info on basic fingering principles, open chords and barre chords, partial chords and broken-set forms, and more. Great for all guitarists!

_____00695224 ....$19.95

SCALE CHORD RELATIONSHIPS

A GUIDE TO KNOWING WHAT NOTES TO PLAY – AND WHY!
• *by Michael Mueller & Jeff Schroedl*

Scale Chord Relationships teaches players how to determine which scales to play with which chords, so guitarists will never have to fear chord changes again! This book/CD pack explains how to: recognize keys; analyze chord progressions; use the modes; play over nondiatonic harmony; use harmonic and melodic minor scales; use symmetrical scales such as chromatic, whole-tone and diminished scales; incorporate exotic scales such as Hungarian major and Gypsy minor; and much more!

_____00695563 Book/CD Pack...................................$14.95

7-STRING GUITAR

AN ALL-PURPOSE REFERENCE FOR NAVIGATING YOUR FRETBOARD
• *by Andy Martin*

Introducing *7-String Guitar*, the first-ever method book written especially for seven-stringed instruments. It teaches chords, scales and arpeggios, all as they are adapted for the 7-string guitar. It features helpful fingerboard charts, and riffs & licks in standard notation and tablature to help players expand their sonic range in any style of music. It also includes an introduction by and biography of the author, tips on how to approach the book, a guitar notation legend, and much more!

_____00695508 ....$12.95

TOTAL ROCK GUITAR

A COMPLETE GUIDE TO LEARNING ROCK GUITAR • *by Troy Stetina*

Total Rock Guitar is a unique and comprehensive source for learning rock guitar, designed to develop both lead and rhythm playing. This book/CD pack covers: getting a tone that rocks; open chords, power chords and barre chords; riffs, scales and licks; string bending, strumming, palm muting, harmonics and alternate picking; all rock styles; and much more. The examples in the book are in standard notation with chord grids and tablature, and the CD includes full-band backing for all 22 songs.

_____00695246 Book/CD Pack....................$17.95

THE GUITAR F/X COOKBOOK

• *by Chris Amelar*

The ultimate source for guitar tricks, effects, and other unorthodox techniques. This book demonstrates and explains 45 incredible guitar sounds using common stomp boxes and a few unique techniques, including: pick scraping, police siren, ghost slide, church bell, jaw harp, delay swells, looping, monkey's scream, cat's meow, race car, pickup tapping, and much more.

_____00695080 Book/CD Pack....................$14.95

BLUES YOU CAN USE

• *by John Ganapes*

A comprehensive source designed to help guitarists develop both lead and rhythm playing. Covers: Texas, Delta, R&B, early rock and roll, gospel, blues/rock and more. Includes 21 complete solos; chord progressions and riffs; turnarounds; moveable scales and more. CD features leads and full band backing.

_____00695007 Book/CD Pack....................$19.95

JAZZ RHYTHM GUITAR

THE COMPLETE GUIDE • *by Jack Grassel*

This book/CD pack by award-winning guitarist and distinguished teacher Jack Grassel will help rhythm guitarists better understand: chord symbols and voicings; comping styles and patterns; equipment, accessories and set-up; the fingerboard; chord theory; and much more. The accompanying CD includes 74 full-band tracks.

_____00695654 Book/CD Pack....................$19.95

FOR MORE INFORMATION, SEE YOUR LOCAL MUSIC DEALER, OR WRITE TO:

HAL•LEONARD®
CORPORATION

7777 W. BLUEMOUND RD. P.O. BOX 13819 MILWAUKEE, WI 53213

Visit Hal Leonard Online at
www.halleonard.com

PRICES, CONTENTS AND AVAILABILITY
SUBJECT TO CHANGE WITHOUT NOTICE.

GUITAR *signature licks*

Signature Licks book/CD packs provide a step-by-step breakdown of "right from the record" riffs, licks, and solos so you can jam along with your favorite bands. They contain performance notes and an overview of each artist's or group's style, with note-for-note transcriptions in notes and tab. The CDs feature full-band demos at both normal and slow speeds.

AEROSMITH 1973-1979
00695106 Book/CD Pack..........$22.95

AEROSMITH 1979-1998
00695219 Book/CD Pack..........$22.95

BEST OF CHET ATKINS
00695752 Book/CD Pack..........$22.95

THE BEACH BOYS DEFINITIVE COLLECTION
00695683 Book/CD Pack..........$22.95

BEST OF THE BEATLES FOR ACOUSTIC GUITAR
00695453 Book/CD Pack..........$22.95

THE BEATLES BASS
00695283 Book/CD Pack..........$22.95

THE BEATLES FAVORITES
00695096 Book/CD Pack..........$24.95

THE BEATLES HITS
00695049 Book/CD Pack..........$24.95

BEST OF ACOUSTIC GUITAR
00695640 Book/CD Pack..........$19.95

BEST OF AGGRO-METAL
00695592 Book/CD Pack..........$19.95

BEST OF GEORGE BENSON
00695418 Book/CD Pack..........$22.95

THE BEST OF BLACK SABBATH
00695249 Book/CD Pack..........$22.95

BEST OF BLINK 182
00695704 Book/CD Pack..........$22.95

BEST OF JAZZ GUITAR
00695586 Book/CD Pack..........$24.95

BEST OF ROCK 'N' ROLL GUITAR
00695559 Book/CD Pack..........$19.95

BEST OF SOUTHERN ROCK
00695560 Book/CD Pack..........$19.95

BLUES GUITAR CLASSICS
00695177 Book/CD Pack..........$19.95

BLUES/ROCK GUITAR MASTERS
00695348 Book/CD Pack..........$17.95

BEST OF CHARLIE CHRISTIAN
00695584 Book/CD Pack..........$22.95

THE BEST OF ERIC CLAPTON
00695038 Book/CD Pack..........$24.95

ERIC CLAPTON – THE BLUESMAN
00695040 Book/CD Pack..........$22.95

ERIC CLAPTON – FROM THE ALBUM UNPLUGGED
00695250 Book/CD Pack..........$24.95

THE BEST OF CREAM
00695251 Book/CD Pack..........$22.95

DEEP PURPLE – GREATEST HITS
00695625 Book/CD Pack..........$22.95

THE DOORS
00695373 Book/CD Pack $22.95

FAMOUS ROCK GUITAR SOLOS
00695590 Book/CD Pack..........$19.95

BEST OF FOO FIGHTERS
00695481 Book/CD Pack..........$22.95

GREATEST GUITAR SOLOS OF ALL TIME
00695301 Book/CD Pack $19.95

BEST OF GRANT GREEN
00695591 Book/CD Pack..........$22.95

GUITAR INSTRUMENTAL HITS
00695309 Book/CD Pack..........$19.95

GUITAR RIFFS OF THE '60S
00695218 Book/CD pack..........$19.95

THE BEST OF GUNS N' ROSES
00695183 Book/CD Pack $22.95

HARD ROCK SOLOS
00695591 Book/CD Pack..........$19.95

JIMI HENDRIX
00696560 Book/CD Pack $24.95

HOT COUNTRY GUITAR
00695580 Book/CD Pack..........$19.95

ERIC JOHNSON
00699317 Book/CD Pack..........$22.95

ROBERT JOHNSON
00695264 Book/CD Pack..........$22.95

ESSENTIAL ALBERT KING
00695713 Book/CD Pack..........$22.95

B.B. KING – THE DEFINITIVE COLLECTION
00695635 Book/CD Pack..........$22.95

THE KINKS
00695553 Book/CD Pack..........$22.95

MARK KNOPFLER
00695178 Book/CD Pack $22.95

BEST OF YNGWIE MALMSTEEN
00695669 Book/CD Pack..........$22.95

BEST OF PAT MARTINO
00695632 Book/CD Pack..........$22.95

MEGADETH
00695041 Book/CD Pack..........$22.95

WES MONTGOMERY
00695387 Book/CD Pack..........$22.95

BEST OF NIRVANA
00695483 Book/CD Pack..........$24.95

VERY BEST OF OZZY OSBOURNE
00695431 Book/CD Pack..........$22.95

BEST OF JOE PASS
00695730 Book/CD Pack..........$22.95

PINK FLOYD – EARLY CLASSICS
00695566 Book/CD Pack..........$22.95

THE POLICE
00695724 Book/CD Pack..........$22.95

THE GUITARS OF ELVIS
00696507 Book/CD Pack..........$22.95

BEST OF QUEEN
00695097 Book/CD Pack..........$22.95

BEST OF RAGE AGAINST THE MACHINE
00695480 Book/CD Pack $22.95**THE**

RED HOT CHILI PEPPERS
00695173 Book/CD Pack..........$22.95

BEST OF DJANGO REINHARDT
00695660 Book/CD Pack..........$22.95

THE ROLLING STONES
00695079 Book/CD Pack..........$22.95

THE BEST OF JOE SATRIANI
00695216 Book/CD Pack..........$22.95

BEST OF SILVERCHAIR
00695488 Book/CD Pack..........$22.95

ROD STEWART
00695663 Book/CD Pack..........$22.95

BEST OF SYSTEM OF A DOWN
00695788 Book/CD Pack..........$22.95

STEVE VAI
00673247 Book/CD Pack..........$22.95

STEVE VAI – ALIEN LOVE SECRETS: THE NAKED VAMPS
00695223 Book/CD Pack..........$22.95

STEVE VAI – FIRE GARDEN: THE NAKED VAMPS
00695166 Book/CD Pack..........$22.95

STEVE VAI – THE ULTRA ZONE: NAKED VAMPS
00695684 Book/CD Pack..........$22.95

STEVIE RAY VAUGHAN
00699316 Book/CD Pack..........$24.95

THE GUITAR STYLE OF STEVIE RAY VAUGHAN
00695155 Book/CD Pack..........$24.95

THE WHO
00695561 Book/CD Pack..........$22.95

BEST OF ZZ TOP
00695738 Book/CD Pack..........$22.95

FOR MORE INFORMATION, SEE YOUR LOCAL MUSIC DEALER, OR WRITE TO:

HAL•LEONARD® CORPORATION
7777 W. BLUEMOUND RD. P.O. BOX 13819 MILWAUKEE, WI 53213

www.halleonard.com

Prices, contents and availability subject to change without notice.

GUITAR PLAY-ALONG

INCLUDES TAB

The Guitar Play-Along Series will help you play your favorite songs quickly and easily. Just follow the tab and listen to the CD to hear how the guitar should sound, and then play along using the separate backing tracks. Mac or PC users can also slow down the tempo by using the CD in their computer. The melody and lyrics are also included in the book in case you want to sing, or to simply help you follow along. 8 songs in each book.

VOLUME 1 – ROCK GUITAR
Day Tripper • Message in a Bottle • Refugee • Shattered • Sunshine of Your Love • Takin' Care of Business • Tush • Walk This Way.
_____00699570 Book/CD Pack $12.95

VOLUME 2 – ACOUSTIC GUITAR
Angie • Behind Blue Eyes • Best of My Love • Blackbird • Dust in the Wind • Layla • Night Moves • Yesterday.
_____00699569 Book/CD Pack $12.95

VOLUME 3 – HARD ROCK
Crazy Train • Iron Man • Living After Midnight • Rock You like a Hurricane • Round and Round • Smoke on the Water • Sweet Child O' Mine • You Really Got Me.
_____00699573 Book/CD Pack..........................$14.95

VOLUME 4 – POP/ROCK
Breakdown • Crazy Little Thing Called Love • Hit Me with Your Best Shot • I Want You to Want Me • Lights • R.O.C.K. in the U.S.A. (A Salute to 60's Rock) • Summer of '69 • What I like About You.
_____00699571 Book/CD Pack..........................$12.95

VOLUME 5 – MODERN ROCK
Aerials • Alive • Bother • Chop Suey! • Control • Last Resort • Take a Look Around (Theme from "M:I-2") • Wish You Were Here.
_____00699574 Book/CD Pack..........................$12.95

VOLUME 6 – '90S ROCK
Are You Gonna Go My Way • Come Out and Play • I'll Stick Around • Know Your Enemy • Man in the Box • Outshined • Smells like Teen Spirit • Under the Bridge.
_____00699572 Book/CD Pack..........................$12.95

VOLUME 7 – BLUES GUITAR
All Your Love (I Miss Loving) • Born Under a Bad Sign • Hide Away • I'm Tore Down • I'm Your Hoochie Coochie Man • Pride and Joy • Sweet Home Chicago • The Thrill Is Gone.
_____00699575 Book/CD Pack..........................$12.95

VOLUME 8 – ROCK
All Right Now • Black Magic Woman • Get Back • Hey Joe • Layla • Love Me Two Times • Won't Get Fooled Again • You Really Got Me.
_____00699585 Book/CD Pack..........................$12.95

VOLUME 9 – PUNK ROCK
All the Small Things • Fat Lip • Flavor of the Weak • Hash Pipe • I Feel So • Pretty Fly (For a White Guy) • Say It Ain't So • Self Esteem.
_____00699576 Book/CD Pack..........................$12.95

VOLUME 10 – ACOUSTIC
Have You Ever Really Loved a Woman? • Here Comes the Sun • The Magic Bus • Norwegian Wood (This Bird Has Flown) • Space Oddity • Spanish Caravan • Tangled up in Blue • Tears in Heaven.
_____00699586 Book/CD Pack..........................$12.95

VOLUME 11 – EARLY ROCK
Fun, Fun, Fun • Hound Dog • Louie, Louie • No Particular Place to Go • Oh, Pretty Woman • Rock Around the Clock • Under the Boardwalk • Wild Thing.
_____00699579 Book/CD Pack..........................$12.95

VOLUME 12 – POP/ROCK
Every Breath You Take • I Wish It Would Rain • Money for Nothing • Rebel, Rebel • Run to You • Ticket to Ride • Wonderful Tonight • You Give Love a Bad Name.
_____00699587 Book/CD Pack..........................$12.95

VOLUME 13 – FOLK ROCK
Leaving on a Jet Plane • Suite: Judy Blue Eyes • Take Me Home, Country Roads • This Land Is Your Land • Time in a Bottle • Turn! Turn! Turn! (To Everything There Is a Season) • You've Got a Friend • You've Got to Hide Your Love Away.
_____00699581 Book/CD Pack..........................$12.95

VOLUME 14 – BLUES ROCK
Blue on Black • Crossfire • Cross Road Blues (Crossroads) • The House Is Rockin' • La Grange • Move It on Over • Roadhouse Blues • Statesboro Blues.
_____00699582 Book/CD Pack..........................$14.95

VOLUME 15 – R&B
Ain't Too Proud to Beg • Brick House • Get Ready • I Can't Help Myself (Sugar Pie, Honey Bunch) • I Got You (I Feel Good) • I Heard It Through the Grapevine • My Girl • Shining Star.
_____00699583 Book/CD Pack..........................$12.95

VOLUME 16 – JAZZ
All Blues • Black Orpheus • Bluesette • Footprints • Misty • Satin Doll • Stella by Starlight • Tenor Madness.
_____00699584 Book/CD Pack..........................$12.95

VOLUME 17 – COUNTRY
All My Rowdy Friends Are Coming over Tonight • Amie • Boot Scootin' Boogie • Chattahoochee • Folsom Prison Blues • Friends in Low Places • T-R-O-U-B-L-E • Workin' Man Blues.
_____00699588 Book/CD Pack..........................$12.95

VOLUME 18 – ACOUSTIC ROCK
About a Girl • Breaking the Girl • Drive • Iris • More Than Words • Patience • Silent Lucidity • 3 AM.
_____00699577 Book/CD Pack..........................$14.95

VOLUME 19 – SOUL
Get up (I Feel like Being) a Sex Machine • Green Onions • In the Midnight Hour • Knock on Wood • Mustang Sally • (Sittin' On) the Dock of the Bay • Soul Man • Walkin' the Dog.
_____00699578 Book/CD Pack..........................$12.95

VOLUME 20 – ROCKABILLY
Blue Suede Shoes • Bluejean Bop • Hello Mary Lou • Little Sister • Mystery Train • Rock This Town • Stray Cat Strut • That'll Be the Day.
_____00699580 Book/CD Pack..........................$12.95

VOLUME 21 – YULETIDE GUITAR PLAY-ALONG
Angels We Have Heard on High • Away in a Manger • Deck the Hall • The First Noel • Go, Tell It on the Mountain • Jingle Bells • Joy to the World • O Little Town of Bethlehem.
_____00699602 Book/CD Pack..........................$12.95

VOLUME 22 – CHRISTMAS GUITAR PLAY-ALONG
The Christmas Song (Chestnuts Roasting on an Open Fire) • Frosty the Snow Man • Happy Xmas (War Is Over) • Here Comes Santa Claus (Right down Santa Claus Lane) • Jingle-Bell Rock • Merry Christmas, Darling • Rudolph the Red-Nosed Reindeer • Silver Bells.
_____00699600 Book/CD Pack..........................$12.95

Prices, contents, and availability subject to change without notice.

FOR MORE INFORMATION, SEE YOUR LOCAL MUSIC DEALER,
OR WRITE TO:

HAL•LEONARD®
CORPORATION
7777 W. BLUEMOUND RD. P.O. BOX 13819 MILWAUKEE, WI 53213

Visit Hal Leonard online at www.halleonard.com

0304